Chris O'Connell

Post and Perimeter Play

Published by:

Reedy Press
PO Box 5131
St. Louis, MO
63139

For more information, please visit our website
at www.reedypress.com, or call us at 1-866-809-9420.

Library of Congress Control Number: on file

ISBN: 978-1-933370-77-4

Printed in the United States of America
08 09 10 11 12 5 4 3 2 1

Contents

Post Play

Post Positioning

There are some key techniques that must become habit for a player to make his or her living in the post.

A good post player must become the **ideal target** for potential entry passes. To do this, the player must incorporate footwork, widening of the body, and recognition that the defender's positioning affects where the player would like to receive the ball.

"L" Targets

When a defender is playing behind, the player should give **"L" Targets** (see Figure 1). This means that elbows are extended wide, and hands are high and facing the ball. The shape of the arm from hand to shoulder looks like the letter *L*.

If a post player, or post, simply extends his or her arms toward the ball, the player is only as wide as his or her shoulders. For a defender to slip in front of a post, the defender needs only to slip around either shoulder. If a post is giving "L"s, the defender has much more width to negotiate to get at the pass.

If a post player feels the defender trying to sneak around the right "L," the post uses that "L" to fend off the defender and the left "L" to give to the passer as a target. The opposite is true should a defender try to sneak around the left "L."

FIGURE 1, L TARGETS

FIGURE 2, FEET CATCHES

Rides

We like to give a **ride** to an aggressive defender. If the defender is sneaking around the high shoulder, or "L," we will move our feet to push the defender in the direction of his or her momentum. This opens up more room on the opposite side, or "L," for the passer to enter the ball away from the defender.

Feet Catches

Feet catches (see Figure 2), or catching the ball with one's feet is an important habit for post players to develop. A post should never wait for a pass to hit his or her hands. Rather, the post should run his or her hands into the ball. We always try to meet passes with out feet moving in direction toward the basketball. If you are waiting for a pass with feet planted to the ground, there is a great chance that the defender will use his or her feet to gain an advantage on the ball. A good post player gives the defender a ride, or steps toward the ball to catch it.

I find myself reminding players to fend off the defender until the ball is catchable. If we stop fending off our defender when the passer releases the ball, we've stopped working, and the defender may have continued.

Halo Passes

Passes lobbed over a fronting defender are called **halo passes** (see Figure 3). To catch these passes successfully, the offensive player must hold position against the defender until the ball goes above the post's own head (like a halo). If the post releases off the defender toward the basket before the ball is catchable, the fronting defender also has room to release and to backpedal to deflect or steal the pass.

FIGURE 3, HALO PASS

Post Positioning Drills

3 Catches

One-on-one in the key (no basket) with a passer at the top or a passer on each wing.

- Offense has to get 3 catches without the defender touching the ball (coaches can defend with use of a football pad).

- The offensive player must catch, pass back, and re-post until catching 3 in a row.

- The post must come to the pass and fend off the defender, who can be aggressive within reason, to succeed in this drill.

Post Moves

I believe strongly in the shot-fake, particularly at the younger levels. Kids naturally love to jump to block their opponent's shot, even though in most cases the defender's best bet would be to stay down, *contest* the shot, and box out.

I've asked all of my coaches to slightly change the name of the *shot-fake* to the **lift-fake** (see Figure 4) and for two reasons:

1. We are trying to *lift* the defender's knees; either the defender unbends his or her knees and stands straight up, or he or she literally jumps up off the floor.

2. Kids' version of an uncoached shot-fake tends to be an unrealistic, rushed, three-inch upward motioning with the basketball. This is not what the beginning of an actual shot looks like.

To solve these problems, we give our kids a rule for their lift-fake: the ball must cross the defender's eyes. This means the ball must travel upward long enough to tempt the defender to come up from his or her stance. Our players are also taught to keep their base from their hips on down during the act of a lift-fake.

Once the defender is lifted and/or airborne, it's imperative that our next offensive step is direct. We prefer to step over one of the defender's feet, which eliminates the defender's chances of sliding sideways to cut off our path once the defender lands. If the defender represented the 12 on a clock, our first step should be toward the 11 or the 1 near the defender but also in a direct route to the basket. Should the player step toward 9 or 3, it gives the defender a window of room to recover upon landing.

FIGURE 4, LIFT-FAKE

Up-and-Under

During an **up-and-under** move, the offensive player faces up, lift-fakes, and steps over the defender's foot in a direct path to the basket. I prefer that my players not spend their dribble prior to the lift. I encourage them instead to use one power dribble to elongate their stride as they step past lifted defenders.

Dribble Counter

In a **dribble counter,** the offensive player catches the ball with his or her back to the basket. The player is attempting to pull the defender toward the middle of the key, both with a turn of the head over his or her inside shoulder and by the direction of one dribble toward the inside. As the defender's footwork takes the defender inside toward the middle of the key, the offensive player drop-steps with the outside foot, trying to point that foot toward the backboard, the target, for our ensuing lay-up shot.

In one motion, the player spins to the outside, pivoting on the newly placed outside foot, and lays the ball off the glass.

I tell my players to think of how they would score on that catch if there were no defender. Surely they would just turn to the outside and lay the ball in. But since there is normally a defender tucked in behind us on the catch, we must pull the defender from that desirable path, so that we may then use it.

If we have a good jump hook from the middle of the key, and our defender knows this and must respect our inside turn and bounce, the dribble counter can be a lethal move.

JUMP HOOK (see Figures 5 and 6)

Players of equal size have a hard time scoring against each other near the basket. If a 6'0" player squares up to the basket facing another 6'0" player shoulder to shoulder, the ball isn't going to make it past the outstretched arms of the defender. We shoot the **jump hook** with a "front shoulder and a back shoulder." If a defender is standing with his or her back to the basket, we put our shoulders perpendicular to the defender's. This means, on a right-handed jump hook, that my left (front) shoulder is on or near the center of the defender's chest, which puts my right (back) shoulder as far away as possible from the defender. So I want to place the ball above that back shoulder and near my ear.

FIGURE 5, JUMP HOOK PRE-SHOT

Now, with some space (the width of my shoulders) between the ball and the defender, I should be able to jump and release the ball off the back shoulder in a manner that makes the shot unblockable. It's crucial that I jump and use the power of my legs to release the ball, preferably at the highest point. I want to avoid twisting in mid-air and squaring up my shoulders to the defender's shoulders. This exposes the ball again, making it likely that the defender will block or change the shot. I want to land similar to the way I jumped, with a front shoulder and a back shoulder.

FIGURE 6, JUMP HOOK

POST MOVE DRILLS

We will use a few props to emphasize certain techniques necessary for effective post moves.

HULA-HOOP DRILL

In an unperfected version of a jump hook, the player will release the ball outside of his or her body. The ball isn't above the back shoulder where the player can use his or her legs to power the release; instead, it's wide and outside of his or her back shoulder, and the player is using only the arm to "throw" the shot.

One of our program's inexpensive training tools is the **hula-hoop**. Our players assume a front-shoulder back-shoulder position with the ball above the back shoulder. The diameter of the hoop is not much larger than the actual player, so the hoop forces the player to keep the ball in the proper position and to jump due north to ensure that the legs, in fact, start the shot. You can raise or lower the hula-hoop to correspond with the desired release point of your players, taking into consideration their height and jumping ability.

Football Pad Drill

A common **football pad** that a coach can slip an arm behind can be used to provide some contact in many drills.

- For the dribble counter, we have the offensive player turn to the middle until the player feels contact from the coach (defender) applying the pad. This contact signifies that the defender has respected the inside dribble and head-fake, and it initiates the counter portion of the move.

- We use the pad similarly for the up-and-under, letting the coaches land with their pad coming down into the offensive player. The player is to drop his or her hips and launch upward, not avoiding contact but securing a trip to the free-throw line against the vulnerable, airborne defender.

ONE-ON-ONE IN THE POST

Since these post moves work best when used in conjunction with each other (the jump hook can set up the dribble counter, etc.), we often play one-on-one in the post in one "super" drill where all post moves are fair game.

- We place a passer on each of the wings and have an offensive player oppose a defender in the post. The ball can move from passer to passer, which changes the entry angles and the defender's positioning. The post player can also pass back to a wing and re-post. We encourage the passers on the wing to use one dribble if it betters the angle where they can enter the ball.

- The two posts generally play to three baskets total. We play "keeps"—if the offensive player scores, the player can immediately recover the ball, pass it to a wing, and re-post for another possession. This drill teaches our posts how to seal a defender on a wing-to-wing skip pass. It also shows how to seal a fronting defender and how to pin down a defender who is playing behind us.

- A fifth player can be added to the drill as a "dig-down defender." This defender is positioned near the top of the free-throw line. Upon a post catch, he will apply double-team pressure to the ball in varying degrees. Sometimes he will simply take a swipe at the ball and return to the perimeter. Other times he will fully trap the ball with the post defender. This forces our offensive posts to move quickly and with a purpose. If they intend to dribble the ball in the paint, it should only be one bounce and it should be a power dribble (low to the ground and two-handed). In varsity games, the post is a high-traffic area. You cannot afford to pause the ball. *An indecisive, unaggressive post player will not survive.*

REBOUNDING

Defensively, there is one important lesson young rebounders should learn: It isn't your job to *get* the rebound; it is your job to *prevent your man* from getting the rebound.

How often do we see a young player aggressively run toward the rim while the shot is in flight? This may appear to be good hustle, but the player is putting himself in poor position to receive a favorable carom. Kids like to run under the basket, but that is where made field goals land—not the misses.

Poor rebounders wait until the ball hits the rim before they begin to block out their man. It is best to do the work while the shot is in flight. Defensively, we simply want to stop the offensive rebounder's momentum, ideally before that player can get any true acceleration. This is why we want to step into the offensive player at the point of contact. Do not let your man get a running start and then try to stop the momentum as he or she crashes into you. Be the one who *delivers* the contact.

Also, avoid turning your backside to a charging offensive rebounder before contact has been made. Once you've turned backward, you've become slower and weaker. I want my players to make the first contact while they are facing their man. I compare it to a left offensive tackle pass-protecting for the quarterback. Make the first contact with an armbar. Once you've slowed the attempt to accelerate past and you are maintaining contact, reverse pivot and get the player on your back. If we do this work while the shot is in flight, we can then go toward the basketball as it caroms toward us. Ideally, we want to catch the rebound at the highest point possible and bring it down to "chin" the ball.

REBOUNDING DRILLS

Place three or four defensive players in the lower half of the key, and their offensive counterparts on the perimeter. When the coach shoots, the defensive players must go out to get their players. ("Get his body first, and the ball second.") You can assign points to the defense or make them secure three in a row, etc. You want to reward the offense as well to ensure that they go hard, as if it were a game. Sometimes I will give the defense an extra player who starts high on the perimeter and make the rule that only that player can secure the rebound for the defense. This is a game-like situation, because often the offense won't send all five to the offensive glass. Also, it forces the bigs on defense to worry solely about boxing out their own man and not worry about the ball. ("It isn't your job to get the rebound; it is your job to prevent your man from getting the rebound.")

Note: There have been times when we've played a team who had one dominant athlete and rebounder. Sometimes a player has to spend all night fighting off that star, while other teammates get all the rebounding glory.

Another effective drill is to leave the defense one man short. Make them identify who on offense has crashed the glass and needs to be boxed off. Also, we must rotate defensively to those closest to the basket. Perhaps you were standing near an offensive wing player, but there is an offensive player unguarded near the basket. That defensive player must rotate down toward the basket to box out that offensive player, because he or she is in a more dangerous position. If a defensive player is guilty of watching the shot in flight before engaging in contact with another body, that player will be badly exposed in this drill.

Perimeter Play

PASSING AND CATCHING

All coaches draw up great plays on their dry-erase board. I've never drawn something up with a marker that, in theory, didn't work. But if the players aren't equipped to execute what you've drawn, it matters very little. I believe passing and catching are fundamentals highly underemphasized by coaches undervalued by players.

We have a simple rule for every pass we attempt in a practice or game: You can only attempt a pass after you have made eye contact with the receiver and that receiver has provided a hand target.

The hand target is important—it signifies that the receiver is ready to handle the pass. When you screen a lot on offense, as we do, it is likely that some passes will get tossed in the direction of a player attempting to screen. You can eliminate many of these adventurous passes by emphasizing the above rule.

An effective hand target is one that tells your teammate not only that you are ready, but it also indicates where you are heading (see Figure 7). As a passer you want to throw the ball where your teammate is going, not where he or she has already been. In addition, we throw passes to the outside of the defense (see Figure 8). If a player was trying to get open on the wing, you wouldn't throw the pass between the player and the defender, you would throw it to the outside, where only that teammate could make the catch.

Think about how much better it is to throw the ball out of bounds than to throw it to the other team. If the ball goes out of bounds, all five players can get back on defense and play straight up. If the defense steals a wing pass, it may take the ball in 1-on-0, or 2-on-1, for an easy conversion. If you only allow the opposition the opportunity to score in 5-on-5 sets, winning will happen.

FIGURE 7, HAND TARGET

FIGURE 8, OUTSIDE TARGET (PASS RECEIVER)

PASSING AND CATCHING DRILLS

We have labeled our passing-and-catching drills "Ball Toughness" drills. We have made "BT" our mantra when it comes to handling pressure and executing on the offensive end. These drills have several variations.

FULL COURT NO DRIBBLE

This is a great conditioner. We will play 5-on-5 full court starting with a jump ball. First team to three baskets wins. I usually only allow a dribble if it leads to a shot. This drill forces players to move without the ball, to come toward the ball with their feet angling against their defender (a good defense will always deny straight line routes). It also emphasizes that players without the ball communicate with a hand target (fingers of the hand target point toward the direction of your momentum). Lead passes can lead to baskets—and to screeners freeing up a teammate who doesn't yet have the ball.

3-on-3 Inside the 3-Point Line

We play 3-on-3 in various ways, sometimes disregarding the basket and making the object to complete eight passes without the defense getting a deflection. Treat the 3-point line as out of bounds, which forces the offensive players to use technique to get open within the scoring area. We teach the thrust step to get open on the wing, walk your man in, making the defender respect a possible back-cut or post-up, and thrust your inside foot across the defender's feet (making your highest foot higher on the court than the defender's). Now you have a head start to pop back to the wing area with your outside target.

2-on-1 Inside the Key

This is basically a game of keep-away. The free-throw line and lane lines are out of bounds, so there is limited space to work with. Any deflection by the defender is a turnover. Emphasize to your offensive players to take a pass to make a pass. You can pass-fake over the defender to get the defender's hands up, then counter by dropping your hips and delivering a bounce pass, etc. You may use your dribble to improve the passing angle available.

Screening and Off-Ball Movement

Ball Screen

It is imperative that your players can read a **ball screen.** We all have a play that calls for a screen on the ball handler, but kids have to understand that the defense can defend that screen in various ways. Does the opposition trap ball screens? Do their players help and recover? Do they go over or under the screener?

It's important to set the ball screen in an area of the court where both screener and ball handler can score from the "scoring area." If the screener sets the ball screen 40 feet away from the basket, it applies little pressure to the defenders involved, because the screener and ball handler aren't in an area they can score from.

Offensively it can pay dividends to screen using two players of unequal sizes. It's much easier to switch on a ball screen that involves two players of roughly the same size and skill.

We like our screeners to screen downhill (see Figures 9 and 10). This means that instead of screening with your body squared to the sideline, the screener angles his or her body so that once the ball handler passes the screener, the ball handler is already headed in the direction of the basket not the sideline. For instance, if the screen is to be set just off-center of the top of the key, our screener's chest will be squared up to the corner of the half-court line and the sideline. The screener's back would conversely be squared to the opposite and diagonal corner where the sideline and baseline meet. Our ball handlers can really "turn the corner" and penetrate to the basket if our screens are set correctly.

If the screener's defender hedges out to help defend the ball momentarily, we ask our ball handlers to string out the helper. This means that the ball handler continues his or her dribble away from the screener to create as much distance as possible from the screener and the screener's defender, who is helping guard the ball at this point. Should the defensive players switch assignments, we may now have a "little" guarding a "big" and vice versa. This is great opportunity to post up the big.

FIGURE 9, PROPER DOWNHILL SCREEN (BALL
HANDLER IS HEADED TOWARD THE BASKET)

FIGURE 10, IMPROPER DOWNHILL SCREEN
(BALL HANDLER IS HEADED TOWARD THE SIDE-
LINE, NOT THE BASKET)

Screener-Cutter

We want our players to make reads without the ball being involved in the screen, too. This again requires the offensive player to cut opposite the direction of the defensive help.

With the ball off center near the top of the key, the post will set a back-screen on the wing player. If the wing goes under the screener (baseline side), this will force the post's defender to help down (toward the baseline).

The screener must then make a "secondary cut." The cutter cuts first, the screener cuts second. The secondary cut is opposite the help, so since the help went low, the screener cuts high. The post in this example should cut toward the passer, generally toward the elbow area. The defense probably helped enough to prevent the cutter from being open on the back-screen, but how can that same helper recover from the baseline to the elbow to guard his or her original player?

Penetrate and Pitch

We emphasize making reads on offense. We do run some set plays, but frankly the defense can always take away something from you, or give you a different look defensively than you had in mind when constructing the set play.

As a coach, it's to your advantage to put the ball into the hands of players who can create help situations off the dribble. If the guard can dribble by his or her defender and head for an easy basket, the wing's defender must pull off the wing and help guard the ball handler. The guard, via the dribble, has created a help situation.

It's important that the wing player recognizes how his or her defender helped. If the wing defender stops the dribble by helping up, then the wing should back-cut. Notice that the offensive reaction should be opposite the defensive reaction.

If the wing defender helps across, then the wing player can backpedal a step to further create distance from the defender. This poses a long recovery for the defensive player should the ball be kicked out to the wing. If the wing defender helps down, by running near the basket, the wing player can "circle behind" the ball. This makes the wing open for a quick pitch-back but also pins the defender behind the ball, making a recovery unlikely.

We practice our "Pen and Pitch" routines with our big men—either with a point guard and a post player or a wing and a post. If we have a wing with the ball and a post player near the block:

- Baseline drive: if the post defender helps down to stop the ball, the post takes a step up (butt to free-throw line).

- Top side drive: if post defender helps up, the post drops down a step (butt to baseline).

Ball Handling

Ball handling and shooting are the two individual skills that cannot be practiced enough. We try to enforce the overload principle on many of our drills by playing a lot of 1-on-2 or 2-on-3, putting players at man disadvantages where they will have no choice but to handle the ball in traffic. When going 2-on-3, the dribbler must be good enough to draw an additional defender's help, making the possession 1-on-1 once the dribbler can successfully pass the ball to the teammate.

Ball Handling Drills

2-on-1/1-on-2

Using a portable basket to cut the length of the court in half, two blue jerseys will go one direction on one white jersey. After a rebound, or a made basket, the one white jersey will go back the other way against two defensive blue jerseys. *Note: This drill is fast paced. It not only overloads the lone white jersey, it gives practice to the blue team at 2-on-1 situations, particularly in regard to spacing, finishing, and drawing the lone defender before passing.*

Touchdown

Put two offensive players on the baseline against three defenders. The objective is for the offense to dribble the ball past the opposite baseline (end zone). You can allot a certain amount of time for the offense to get across the line. Since the defense usually elects to trap the ball, we have the second offensive player trail the trap to receive a "lateral" from the teammate. We don't allow forward passes. It's important for players without the ball to recognize traps and to come to the ball in a manner that creates a clean passing lane from the ball to the hand target.

T-DRILL

This drill is slow paced at first but combines ball handling with footwork. Have a player or coach stand facing the offensive player with feet shoulder-width apart and arms extended to the side so that he or she looks like a "T." The offensive player should make an effort to pass the defender close to the defender's body; a route that is too far from the defender allows the defender to step into open space and improve his or her defensive position. If your first offensive step is across the defender's "foot line," the defender won't be able to slide over without fouling you. Likely, the defender's first step will be backward, toward the basket, as the defender opens up his or her body.

Open Step

Right foot takes a short step. You then do two things at once: Start your dribble as your left foot thrusts across the defender's foot line, and your left hip goes just by the defender's left hip.

Cross Step

(see Figures 11 and 12) Right foot crosses over and thrusts past the defender's foot line, as your right hip goes across the defender's right hip.

Figure 11, Cross Step

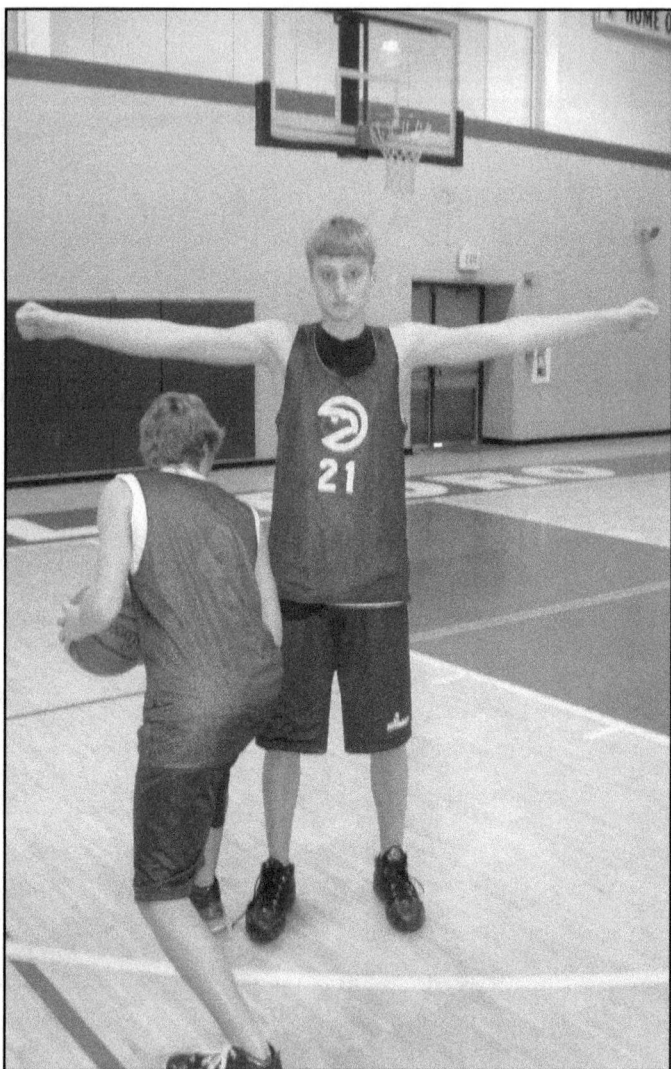

FIGURE 12, CROSS STEP

www.ingramcontent.com/pod-product-compliance
Lightning Source LLC
Chambersburg PA
CBHW060810110426
42739CB00032BA/3165